A Collection of
Random Poetic Rumblings

Isabel G. Isiderio

Illustrated by FlashyCrow and David Isiderio

To my precious son and lil' princess ~
Mommy loves you forever

Thanks Mom and Dad for never giving up on me. I love you.
Thanks Sam, my awesome bro, for believing in my dreams
even when I had forsaken them.
John 3:16
Eternally grateful to my Lord Jesus Christ.

TABLE OF CONTENTS

TABLE OF CONTENTS

DREAMS

Dreams come and dreams go,
In a space where the mind flows;
Vacant and restless in the dark,
Hoping for a moment to spark.

I thought I saw you in my dream,
And I called out to you with a scream —
But you were always far away,
Never for a moment to stay.

And yet I wish the time would come,
When you wouldn't feel so numb;
So that one day you will finally see,
I wrote this poem to set me free.

1

CUPCAKE DIVINE

Cupcake, dearest cupcake, you're so fine
Your sugary confection just blows my mind!
Curse the fact you'll make me fat —
I must honor the sacred belly pact!

To ignore you would only pain me so,
More than your frosty delights will ever know!
Moist chocolate and vanilla gone to waste,
Sprinkles galore escaping my taste!

This luscious craving will be my undoing
Since fitness should be my main pursuin'...
Oh, blast it all! I'll stuff my face —
In secret, greedy, crazy haste!

So when in public, I can politely decline
Those sweet temptations, ever so divine!
For such joys I already devoured and embraced
That now I can refuse with a plumpy moon face!

Infamy and fame seem now all one and the same,

Hordes be ruthless, ignoring all shame;

Just promise them a spark or a glimmer of hope,

That they could be more famous than Saint Nick or the Pope.

Outrageous and cringey deeds are done to achieve,

Whatever it takes for their name to succeed!

Nothing is off limits, just frame their name in lights —

Drowning others is capital to reach their maximum heights.

Morality is distorted in this modern age,

What's good is now bad so lock it in a cage!

Self-entitlement means others are always to blame,

Cuz one's ultimate fame is the name of the game.

BUNNYLAND

Happily escape to the dearest of lands,

Where cuteness overload isn't a sham;

Sweet bunnies greet you with their cute button eyes,

Wiggling their noses at your delighted surprise!

With their plumpy frames and fluffy long ears,

You'll be reduced to nothing but jolly fat tears!

And despite all reservations, you now willingly comply

To bring cartful of carrots, promising a 10-year supply.

4a

With a carefree laugh and a heart full of song,

Bewitched by their cotton tails, you go follow along;

For prisoners of Bunnyland never feel they're ensnared,

The great powers of cuteness has all logic impaired!

To play and care for bunnies is all you'll ever do,

When you escape to Bunnyland, their hearts cling to you.

4b

It Will Never Be

I wish you were here with me,

But it will never be.

I wish we kept those promises,

But it will never be.

Imagine how different life would have been

If we simply made those changes,

And took the time to listen,

If only we had fought with all our might —

Just to make it happen.

Imagine how beautiful it would be

To have you still here...

  To walk this path with me...

    But I know in the end,

      It will never be.

TO
PURPLE
ARMY

They say it'll be a gloomy day
    When BTS members must go away,
Training as other Korean boys must do,
    For military service they're required to pursue.

Army will miss them once they're all gone,
    I heard Jin will be the first to get buff and all strong...
They're not off to wiggle at some grand disco ball,
    It's all to protect their nation from an enemy's overhaul.

So release them I say, it's for a great cause!
    It's better they do their duty and give dancing a pause —
Cuz serving and protecting others is truly what's best,
    For heroes are forged from fires of selflessness.

Now wish them well and say your adieus,
    Maybe give a purple heart and say, "saranghae" too;
As loyalties must sometimes endure a season of test,
    To prove BTS will emerge stronger — A cut above the rest!

WORTH

You're charming and beautiful they often say,
Like the wild flowers that bloom in May.
But do you really believe that's honest and true?
Or are they just being extra nice to you?

You're ever so clever, even a genius some claim,
That you'll graduate with honors and achieve great fame!
But do you really believe that's accurate and true?
Or are those mere compliments just to flatter you?

You're an exquisite talent, they frequently boast;
All your works should be on display and given a grand toast!
But do you really believe that's sincere and true?
Or are they just messin' around with you?

For no matter what opinions others may have,
Be it good or bad or just plain mad!
Don't base your worth on the views of others,
Because this fickle foundation eventually withers.

But believe you are precious in God's holy sight,
Unique and created with much purpose and delight!
For this is the start of accepting a truth so bright,
That it will help guide you through the darkest of nights.

HOMEWORK

Homework, homework, dark and dreary
Never showing any mercy;
The midnight candle burns through the night —
I must stay awake, I must finish the fight!

Eating snacks will do the trick
Fueling up like John Wick!
I must not rest for in a moment...
Sleep will be my greatest opponent!

Daylight is nigh and the time has come —
My head is beating like a drum!
So close the books and iPad too,
And let my eyes shut like crazy glue.

TWITTER²

Twitter, Twitter, what does it matter?

They say Musk has liberals all in tatters!

8 bucks to own that coveted blue check,

To secure your mark in the internet's specs.

Such trouble and fuss over a puny bird's throne —

Selling Tesla stocks instead of investing in cyberclones!

But then again, there's that journey to Mars...

Still a one up against Bezos who barely scrapped the stars.

So what now becomes of Twitter, shall we wait and see?

Come bring out the popcorn and watch with jubilee!

Will free speech be its tone the Founding Fathers had advised?

Or will tyranny and suppression be its ultimate demise?

9

X marks the spot
Where the blue bird once was;
Its disappearance caused quite a buzz
For reasons it undoes.

Not a fluffy feather in sight
Poor birdie vanished into the night;
'Twas a pretty penny to pay they say
For truth to bask in the day.

X now championed a platform for free speech
Even for the falsely accused and impeached;
So will X survive the trial —
To quell those in denial?

Perhaps only time can tell
If Musk still holds an ace or a conjuring spell;
To sway naysayers and doubters
That voices for all generally matters.

NEW YEAR'S RESOLUTION

AUDIT

The new year is here,

Big whoop-de-do.

So, what was it again

That you were planning to do?

Was it the six-pack abs you vowed at the gym?

Perhaps being more patient or finally learning how to swim?

Could it be new music you've longed to compose?

Or simply being brave enough to propose?

Well, whatever it is, just don't forget

You must work up a sweat or set a wise preset.

Because resolutions won't transpire to desired conclusions,

If they only remain as flimsy, wishful illusions.

THE ONE

Secretly hoping he'd see you there,

It's a desperate wish beyond compare!

For you're only one among a sea of fish,

Yet yearning he'd pick you out like a favorite dish.

Amid the screams and teary eyes,

You faintly smile and exhale long sighs.

Why can't he see this damsel in distress?

And save you from sinking in a dungeon of emotional mess?

He laughs and waves with a cheery grin

Saying he loves you all, wondering where you've been;

He enchants the crowd as he plays their heart strings,

With songs that ascend him higher than Cupid's wings.

12 a

But alas, the pricy night must come to a close,

A nightmare diehard fans hate to disclose.

You sob realizing you've spent all your cash

On useless merch in the closet you'll later stash.

Then against all odds, luck, and chance

He politely bows and takes one last glance...

Suddenly noticing you, fair siren of the sea

His Apollo eyes sparkle with curiosity!

You hold your breath and pinch your arm —

Hyperventilating cuz it's not a false alarm!

So now that you'll be plucked from obscurity,

Do you really think you're ready for this new reality?

12 b

Echoes of the Past

If only I could go back to that fateful day,

The echoes of the past would then fade away.

No longer chained to grief and demise,

Nor succumbed to miseries of tragic goodbyes.

Life would be meaningful, not lost in a haze

For the light of your presence will fill up my days;

Rejoicing to see life once more in your eyes,

To marvel at the moon and watch another sun rise.

Having you again is worth far more than gold,

Cherished and more prized than treasures untold;

But now I only see you alive in my dreams,

Where our days together remain evergreen…

The echoes of the past only haunt me anew

Of memories engrained, always ever of you.

COPS

Cops are just not merely blue,

They're black, brown, white, and come in every hue;

They're only human, just like me and you

So cut them some slack cuz perfect isn't what you are too.

Daily risking their lives to serve and protect,

Isn't the path most would like to trek;

The cost so high and the pay rather small,

It's really not the best, most desirable call.

Yes, there's no doubt there are corrupt po-pos,

Just like how there's slimy politicians and CEOs;

But we shouldn't lump and categorize them all

Cuz that's unfair treatment and simply illogical.

So be grateful to the officers who are responsible and true,

To the admirable work they've set out to do!

Cuz without good cops society will be

A Wild West of caped crusaders, each justifying their own vigilante.

14

FASHION and MONEY

To some, fashion is a passion

That becomes their money's grisly assassin;

Always buying without askin'

If they ought to hold back and wisely ration.

You see, there's an underlying itch,

To grab that item without a flinch;

Dictating their conscience that it wasn't a glitch,

That they weren't manipulated by some sales pitch.

So hurry now and smarten up,

And wisely fill your financial cup;

For fancy clothes can't save the day,

When rainy days come to take all your money away!

15

T H E

Mysterious

M O D E L

With killer looks that would make you blink,

And always lookin' fly when he smirks and winks,

With his radiant smile and mesmerizing laugh,

You wish you could have more than an autograph.

He's a mysterious one, perhaps not internationally known;

Yet his face is plastered everywhere as if he's multi-cloned.

And that's because his account isn't properly identified,

So scammers steal, since his true self isn't verified.

16 a

Social media is littered with fake accounts,

Confusing and dividing his followers with great doubts;

Countless profiles all claiming to be,

Posting pics with his watermarks for us to see.

So who is this guy? I'd really like to know —

It's almost like a game the cunning Riddler has bestowed!

Perhaps we need Batman to finally solve this case,

So fans can correctly follow this model dude,

And his ranking in popularity will finally be placed.

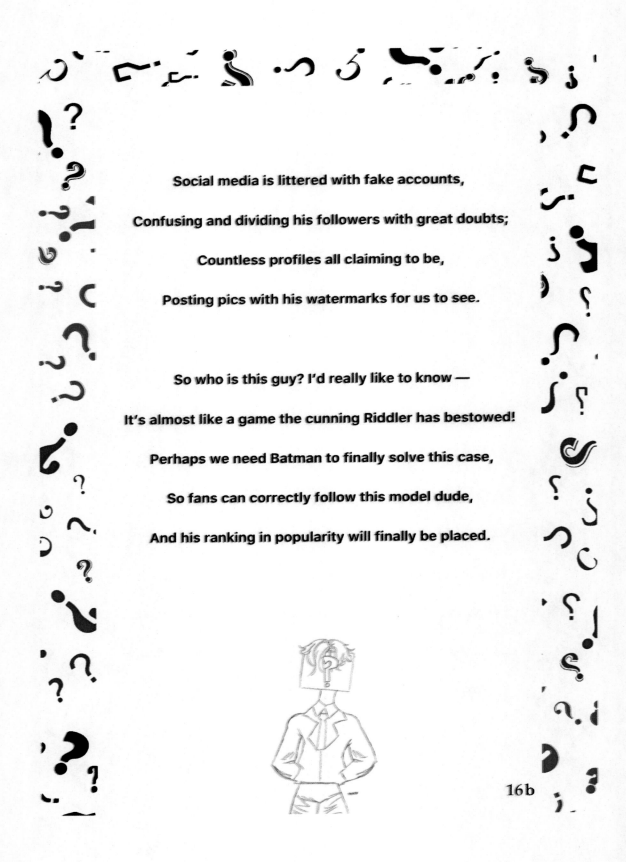

A Tale of Two Bros

In reference to Charles Dickens, I shall begin:

It was the woke of times, it was the broke of times;

Two brothers once strongly united,

Now stand utterly divided.

Maybe it all began over tears and a poofy dress,

Or maybe it was due to years of agony and distress,

That in comparison to the heir's, his rooms were more compressed,

Lacking grandiose views for his personal access.

Why, it's downright outrageous and most horribly unfair —

That the spare be not treated exactly like the heir!

So recollections must vary and family secrets unburied,

Until reparations and apologies be ferried

To the flawless one he married.

So when will the wounds and broken hearts mend?

When will the bitterness and royal circus end?

Will the two bros be ever reunited?

Shall a game of thrones be played for the undecided?

Perhaps peace and harmony will only return,

When millions turn to billions in their clanging money urn;

Or is everybody doomed for the icy London Tower,

If the royal crown's not given to the jealous little brother?

RAIDEN

Tall and slender, sleek and slim

He plays the guitar to its outer rim;

Fierce and heavy in each strum that sings,

Piercing hearts with metallic rings.

Afar and adrift from another realm,

He radiates essence that overwhelms;

Celestial edge and mystical eyes,

Such visage awes to hypnotize.

From deep within his soul to bare,

Dimensions of art — only he would dare;

Near he comes and yet so far,

Strikes beautiful scars with his guitar.

18

UNREQUITED LOVE

He's a famous, sought-after idol

    Yet it's sad to say,

It seems the one he truly wants,

    Always gets away.

Globally he's adored and millions love him so,

    And yet the one he's loved so long, rejects him with a "no."

I guess the lesson here is plain for us to see,

    That even celebs can't have it all, despite who they may be.

So, gentlemen, if you've found your forever love,

    Be good and thank your Father up above;

Because some have searched far and wide,

    And others have waited a lifetime...

        For their never ever bride.

It's Hard

It's hard to be nice when no one cares,

It's hard to be nice when no one shares;

 It's hard to be nice when everything is failing,

It's hard to be nice when everyone's wailing!

I wish they'd just listen whenever I'm talking,

And not make me sit long waiting and staring;

It's really upsetting when no one minds,

That my world right now doesn't seem to shine.

They say I gotta grow up,

And stop being so bratty;

Cuz the world doesn't spin around me

So I shouldn't be so pushy!

20 a

Maybe I'll think about it or maybe I won't,

Maybe being emo is better than a popular vote!

But watchin' the world go by as I sit here alone,

Is turnin' me into a grumpy petrified stone.

Frowning and growling all day is exhausting,

So maybe it's time to start a lil' readjusting:

It's hard to be angry when you choose joy over pain,

It's hard to be angry when you're thankful for the rain.

It's hard to be angry when you spread love and good cheer,

It's hard to be angry when you value others before your own rear!

20b

Seniors

Senior citizens are a lot of fun,

Especially when they've forgotten something they've already done!

You can watch your favorite film with them about a dozen times,

Cuz they'll marvel anew at all the thrills and silly crimes.

Have a pillow ready cuz seniors talk 'til dawn,

Of long ago glories — of all the fun they've done.

You nod your head cuz you've heard 'em a thousand times before,

The miles they walked to school, used rocks for toys —

You'd think they even played with a dinosaur!

Oh, but the wisdom they've gathered and often do convey

From vast experiences, shimmering from their hairs of grey!

These are priceless treasures, we ought to note and collect

For history likes to repeat itself, a fact youths often neglect.

Ignore not the sacrifices seniors had to endure,

For their children and the following generations, better futures they secured.

Cuz often their sacrifices paved the way for comforts we now enjoy,

Through their courage and resilience they determined to employ.

So let's be mindful and treat our seniors with much respect,

Genuinely care, provide, and loyally protect.

Honor and love them, while time still allows

Cuz memories will be all that's left after the final curtain bows.

Le Bizarre

In the world of Le Bizarre
Nothing's near or very far;

The earth's a triangle and trees are flat,
And circles are sharp, as a matter of fact!

You cruise around in jiggly cars,
And fuel 'em with music from flute guitars;

And in this twisted, loony realm,
Only the silliest control the helm!

And no one cares about pricey gems,
Cuz everyone's face is made of them!

Oh, but for cotton candy hair that twirls —
Now those are more valued than fancy pearls!

For in the world of Le Bizarre,
Everyone deserves a shiny star!

CONQUER

A storm is raging through the night,

And it gives me such a fright!

But I must conquer to the end,

My will must never, ever bend!

They say your fears will take control,

But don't you mind, so take a stroll!

The power to win is within your grasp —

Dare your terrors not to clasp!

Just be brave and ever true,

In all you say and think and do;

Thus, in the end you'll never be

Bending the knee to a lousy flea!

One More Miracle

One more miracle
Lord, it's all I ask ...

Just one more miracle,
To amend my broken past.

One more miracle
To get me through this day,

Please, one more miracle
Lord, I humbly pray.

There's nowhere else to turn
To help me change my fate,

The waters are rising
To heights I can't escape.

But if you're willing, Lord,
Another dawn awaits for me;

If only you are willing, Lord,
I will finally be free!

Just one more miracle,
That's all I ask from you;

Please, one more miracle
Of your promises ever true.

You're the only One who can save me,
From the fury of the sea —

Please, have mercy, my God
On this wretched sinner, I plea.

It's Never Too Late

It's never too late to start again,

To hope and dream for a better end;

It's never too late to love once more,

To believe in second chances — go let your heart explore!

It's never too late to rekindle forgotten joys,

To happily laugh like a child with new toys!

It's never too late to feel young once more,

To dance in the rain or seek adventures like before.

Although life is short and nothing is promised,

Cherish what you have and go on — be dauntless!

Indeed, our days are numbered, but as long as you're living,

It's never too late, as long as you're willing.

`Til next time...

Bunnie-Bye

Made in the USA
Las Vegas, NV
06 June 2024